CW00507083

Conversations

on

The Unlikely Pilgrimage of Harold Fry

Rachel Joyce

By dailyBooks

FREE Download: Get the Hottest Books!
*Get Your Free Books with **Any Purchase** of* Conversation Starters!

  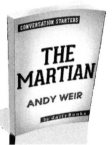

Every purchase comes with a FREE download of the hottest titles!

Add spice to any conversation
Never run out of things to say
Spend time with those you love

Read it for FREE on any smartphone, tablet, Kindle, PC or Mac.
No purchase necessary - licensed for personal enjoyment only.

or Click Here.

Scan Your Phone

Please Note: This is an unofficial conversation starters guide. If you have not yet read the original work, please do so first.

Copyright © 2015 by dailyBooks. All Rights Reserved. First Published in the United States of America 2015

We hope you enjoy this complementary guide from **dailyBooks.** *We aim to provide quality, thought provoking material to assist in your discovery and discussions on some of today's favorite books.*

Disclaimer / Terms of Use: Product names, logos, brands, and other trademarks featured or referred to within this publication are the property of their respective trademark holders and are not affiliated with dailyBooks. The publisher and author make no representations or warranties with respect to the accuracy or completeness of these contents and disclaim all warranties such as warranties of fitness for a particular purpose. This guide is unofficial and unauthorized. It is not authorized, approved, licensed, or endorsed by the original book's author or publisher and any of their licensees or affiliates.

No part of this publication may be reproduced or retransmitted, electronic or mechanical, without the written permission of the publisher.

Tips for Using dailyBooks Conversation Starters:

EVERY GOOD BOOK CONTAINS A WORLD FAR DEEPER THAN the surface of its pages. The characters and their world come alive through the words on the pages, yet the characters and its world still live on. Questions herein are designed to bring us beneath the surface of the page and invite us into the world that lives on. These questions can be used to:

- Foster a deeper understanding of the book
- Promote an atmosphere of discussion for groups
- Assist in the study of the book, either individually or corporately
- Explore unseen realms of the book as never seen before

About Us:

THROUGH YEARS OF EXPERIENCE AND FIELD EXPERTISE, from newspaper featured book clubs to local library chapters, *dailyBooks* can bring your book discussion to life. Host your book party as we discuss some of today's most widely read books.

Table of Contents

Introducing *The Unlikely Pilgrimage of Harold Fry*

THE UNLIKELY PILGRIMAGE OF HAROLD FRY TELLS THE story of Harold, a 65-year-old man living in Kingsbridge, England. Harold receives a letter from an old friend and co-worker, Queenie Hennessy. The letter informs him that Queenie is dying from cancer, and she is staying in a hospice care center. Harold writes back to Queenie, but when he goes to post the letter, he continuously stops himself from mailing it. Instead of sending the letter, Harold decides to pay Queenie a visit at the hospice center. He makes a phone call to the hospice center to let them know he will be coming. Then, he decides to make the entire 600-mile journey on foot.

Whenever Harold makes a stop during his pilgrimage, he sends a postcard to his wife, Queenie, and a young woman that he met at a gas station. Maureen, Harold's wife, is concerned about him taking such a long journey by foot. One day, she realizes that she could simply drive to meet Harold and make sure he is well. When she meets up with Harold, he asks her to join him. She declines the offer; however, she apologizes to him for being selfish by asking him to discontinue his journey.

As Harold walks, he starts to look at his past. He begins working through the issues that have plagued him for years. Prominent issues in Harold's past include his mother abandoning him as a child and his father kicking him out of the house when he was sixteen. He ends up feeling as though he is following in his mother's footsteps. He also begins to confront the issues of his son's death.

At one point in the journey, Harold realizes his bank account is running low on funds; so he buys a sleeping bag and begins sleeping outside and decides to send his debit card and other personal items home. Soon after, the media catches word of his pilgrimage, which leads to numerous people joining Harold on his pilgrimage, which Harold does not like.

Eventually, he reaches the hospice center where Queenie is staying. However, he decides not to see her. He meets up with Maureen, and the two of them spend time together on the beach reconnecting. They go back to the hospice center together and learn that Queenie has died peacefully.

Introducing the Author

RACHEL JOYCE IS AN ENGLISH AUTHOR CURRENTLY LIVING in Gloucestershire, England. Her husband, Paul Venables, is a psychotherapist and actor. They have two children together.

Prior to becoming a writer, Rachel Joyce was an actress. She had the opportunity to work with the Royal Shakespeare Company. When she became pregnant with her first child, she discontinued her career as an actor. Her last play was *Othello,* in which she had to hide her pregnancy under clothes while she was playing the character of Emilia.

After her career as an actress ended, Joyce began writing plays for radio. In 2007, she won the Tinniswood Award for the play she wrote entitled *To Be A Pilgrim.* In 2012, she released her first novel, *The Unlikely Pilgrimage of Harold Fry*. She wrote a companion book to this novel in 2014 called *The Love Song of*

Miss Queenie Hennessey. The first book she wrote as a child was about a family of cats who wore human clothing, which she illustrated herself.

Joyce stated in an interview that she enjoys writing stories about people who live ordinary lives until they suddenly come upon something extraordinary. She believes her story must have an issue that has to be resolved, and this should be pointed out at the beginning of the story. However, the reader should only be given clues rather than have the problem stated bluntly. She also wants her stories to be enjoyed by both readers who do not notice small details and the readers who do.

Rachel Joyce was inspired to be a writer because of the great need she felt to communicate with others. Through writing, Joyce is able to express herself, which is helpful for her because she often feels as though she does not fit in with the world around her. She also enjoys creating something new, and she is able to do that through writing.

Discussion Questions

. . . .

question 1

When Harold gets to the mailbox, he stops and keeps walking.
Why do you think he continues to walk at the mailbox?

. . . .

question 2

Harold stops to talk to a girl at a garage. Her story inspires him to go on his journey. Why do you think she was such a strong inspiration for him?

. . . .

. . . .

question 3

Maureen is firmly against Harold walking to see Queenie.
Eventually, she comes to understand why he has to do it. How
does she come to this understanding?

. . . .

. . . .

question 4

While he is on his journey, Harold gets a lot of attention from the media. What are the benefits of the media coverage? What are the negative parts of having media coverage?

. . . .

. . . .

question 5

At one point in the pilgrimage, Harold gets rid of his map and
other possessions. Why do you think he does this?

. . . .

· ·

question 6

Consider the transformation Harold undergoes throughout his pilgrimage. In what ways does he change from the beginning of the story to the end of the story?

· ·

question 7

Throughout most of the novel, Harold and Maureen have a rocky relationship. Why do you think they stay married?

. . . .

question 8

The title of this novel is *The Unlikely Pilgrimage of Harold Fry.*
Why do you think Rachel Joyce chose to use the word
"pilgrimage" instead of journey in the title? What was "unlikely"
about the pilgrimage?

. . . .

question 9

Consider the relationship between Harold and Maureen. How does their relationship evolve from the beginning of the novel to the end?

question 10

Queenie was the main motivation for Harold to go on the pilgrimage. Why do you think Harold felt so strongly that he had to go to see Queenie instead of just sending her the letter?

. . . .

question 11

Surely, Harold could have taken a bus, train, or car to see
Queenie. Why do you think he chose to make the entire
pilgrimage on foot?

. . . .

question 12

In *The Unlikely Pilgrimage of Harold Fry*, we learn that Harold's son had died tragically. Why do you think it was so difficult for Harold to find closure and peace with his son's death?

· ·

question 13

While Queenie was in hospice, Harold was on a journey to see her. When Harold finally arrived at the hospice center, were you surprised by her condition? What were you hoping would happen when Harold reached Queenie?

· ·

question 14

A waitress in *The Unlikely Pilgrimage of Harold Fry* tells Harold that if people do not "go mad" from time to time, then there would be "no hope." What do you think the waitress meant by this?

question 15

One quote from *The Unlikely Pilgrimage of Harold Fry* says that a person's life can seem ordinary to them only because they have been living the same way for so long. What do you think this quote means?

. . . .

question 16

"Thought provoking" is one phrase that readers used to describe *The Unlikely Pilgrimage of Harold Fry*. Did this book cause you to think about things in your own life?

. . . .

. . . .

question 17

One reader considered *The Unlikely Pilgrimage of Harold Fry* to be sentimental. Did you feel emotional while reading this novel?

. . . .

question 18

It was stated that *The Unlikely Pilgrimage of Harold Fry* would translate well on stage as a play. Do you think this story would be successful as a play or film?

. . . .

question 19

The Unlikely Pilgrimage of Harold Fry is a novel that many readers say they will never be able to forget. Did you find this story unforgettable?

. . . .

. . . .

question 20

Some people have commented that not many people want to read a story about "old people." What are your thoughts on these comments?

. . . .

FREE Download: Get the Hottest Books!
*Get Your Free Books with **Any Purchase** of* Conversation Starters!

Every purchase comes with a FREE download of the hottest titles!

Add spice to any conversation
Never run out of things to say
Spend time with those you love

Read it for FREE on any smartphone, tablet, Kindle, PC or Mac.
No purchase necessary - licensed for personal enjoyment only.

Get it Now

or Click Here.

Scan Your Phone

question 21

The Unlikely Pilgrimage of Harold Fry is a story with an original and uncommon plot according to many readers. Have you read another novel like this one?

. . . .

question 22

Many readers have talked about the "simple" and unembellished writing in *The Unlikely Pilgrimage of Harold Fry*. What were your thoughts on Rachel Joyce's writing?

. . . .

question 23

Readers have called Harold Fry an "unlikely hero." What is meant by the term "unlikely hero," and do you agree with these readers?

. . . .

question 24

One reader stated that they felt satisfied with the ending of the
novel. Do you agree or disagree? How would you have liked to see
the novel end?

. . . .

. . . .

question 25

The Unlikely Pilgrimage of Harold Fry was a quick read for many
people. How did you feel about the pace of the story?

. . . .

question 26

Rachel Joyce stopped her career as an actress to be a writer. Do you think her experience as an actress influenced her writing in any way?

. . . .

. . . .

question 27

Rachel Joyce often feels like an outsider, so she writes to express
herself. Do you think her writing is an effective means of
expression?

. . . .

· ·

question 28

Before becoming a novelist, Rachel Joyce was a playwright for radio. How do you think her experience in writing plays helped her when writing novels?

· ·

question 29

Rachel Joyce believes that a good story should have an issue that must be resolved. Do you agree with her on this statement?

. . . .

question 30

Paul Venables, Rachel Joyce's husband, is a psychotherapist in addition to being an actor. How influential do you think he is to Joyce's writing?

· ·

question 31

Years before this story starts, Queenie went to visit Harold to tell him that she did not blame him. How might the story be different had Maureen passed the message along to Harold?

. . . .

question 32

The journey that Harold takes transforms him in many ways. If he had not gone on this journey, what might Harold's life be like?

question 33

Would you ever embark on a journey like Harold? What do you think would motivate you to take a journey like Harold?

. . . .

question 34

If you were in Harold's position, and you had a choice to either send a letter to an old friend in hospice or visit them one last time, which choice would you make?

· ·

question 35

Harold makes a sudden decision at the mailbox to walk to see
Queenie. Tell about an experience in life where you suddenly
made a life changing decision?

· ·

. . . .

question 36

If Queenie were not so close to death, do you think Harold would still have gone to visit her? Why do you think he waited so long to see her again?

. . . .

. . . .

question 37

Maureen goes to meet up with Harold when he reaches Queenie's hospice center. How do you think the story would have been different if she waited until Harold returned home to speak to him again?

. . . .

. . . .

question 38

Many people accompany Harold on his journey to see Queenie,
which Harold dislikes. If you were making a long journey, would
you prefer to make it alone or have someone with you?

. . . .

Quiz Questions

. . . .

question 39

In *The Unlikely Pilgrimage of Harold Fry*, the main character sets out on a journey to see his old friend, _____, who is dying of cancer.

. . . .

question 40

His wife, _____, is deeply against him taking this journey. However, she later apologizes for trying to stop him.

question 41

When Harold makes a stop on his journey, he sends a
_____. He sends one to his wife, one to
Queenie, and one to a kind stranger.

question 42

True or False: Harold decides to drive to Queenie because this will be the fastest route, and he needs to make it to her on time.

question 43

True or False: Harold struggles with many issues in his past including his mother leaving, his father kicking him out, and his son's death.

question 44

True or False: Harold arrives at the hospice center right before Queenie dies and agrees to sit with her as she passes away.

question 45

True or False: Maureen meets up with Harold at the hospice center. The two of them reconcile and reconnect on the beach, and they laugh together for the first time in years.

question 46

Rachel Joyce is a native of _____. She currently lives there with her husband and their two children.

. . . .

question 47

Before working as a writer, she was an _____.
In this career, she worked with the Royal Shakespeare Company.

. . . .

question 48

Rachel Joyce was a writer of _____ before she became a novelist. She won the Tinniswood Award in 2007 for *To Be A Pilgrim*.

. . . .

question 49

The first novel that Rachel Joyce released was
_____ in 2012. The companion novel for
this story is *The Love Song of Miss Queenie Hennessey*.

question 50

True or False: Rachel Joyce feels the need to communicate with others because she often feels as though she is an outsider in the world. This is part of why she became a writer.

. . . .

Quiz Answers

1. Queenie
2. Maureen
3. postcard
4. False; Harold walks.
5. True
6. False; Harold does not go to visit Queenie.
7. True
8. England
9. actress
10. plays
11. *The Unlikely Pilgrimage of Harold Fry*
12. True

THE END

Want to promote your book group? Register here.

PLEASE LEAVE US A FEEDBACK.

THANK YOU!

FREE Download: Get the Hottest Books!
*Get Your Free Books with **Any Purchase** of* Conversation Starters!

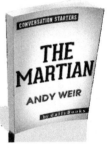

Every purchase comes with a FREE download of the hottest titles!

Add spice to any conversation
Never run out of things to say
Spend time with those you love

Read it for FREE on any smartphone, tablet, Kindle, PC or Mac.
No purchase necessary - licensed for personal enjoyment only.

Get it Now

or Click Here.

Scan Your Phone

Printed in Great Britain
by Amazon

17920382R00041